Environmental
AMERICA

Environmental AMERICA

The Southeastern States

by
D.J. Herda

The Millbrook Press
Brookfield, CT
The American Scene

Cover photographs courtesy of D. J. Herda

Inside photographs courtesy of
Tom Stack & Associates: 8, 44, 47; U.S. Environmental Protection Agency: 15, 16, 18, 22, 24, 27, 39, 41, 50; U.S.D.A. Forest Service, R. W. Neelands: 13; U.S. Department of Energy, 21; D.J. Herda: 8, 10, 19, 30, 33

Designed by Moonlit Ink, Madison, WI 53705
Illustrations by Renee Graef

Cataloging-in-Publication Data
Herda, D. J.
Environmental America: The Southeastern States.
Brookfield, CT, The Millbrook Press. 1991.
64 p.; col. ill.; (The American Scene)
Includes bibliographical references and index.
Summary: The impact of humankind and society on the environment, with special emphasis on the Southeastern region
ISBN 1-878841-07-6   639.9 HER

1. Southeastern states—environmental impacts—juvenile literature. 2. Conservation of natural resources. 3. Pollution. [1. Environmental America: The Southeastern States] I Title. II. Series.

CONTENTS

INTRODUCTION

It may have been mere coincidence that the first two colonies to be settled in the Americas were located along the southeastern seaboard. Or it may have been something more—an attraction to the magnificent beauty, the vast range of wildlife, the endless variety of fruits and vegetables, and protection from the winter snowstorms that took so heavy a toll on those colonies founded in the Northeast.

Whatever the reasons, when Don Pedro Menendez de Aviles chose St. Augustine in present-day Florida for the first permanent European settlement in North America, he made the right choice. Its gently rolling hills, sprawling sandy beaches, and crystal-clear waterways provided the perfect backdrop for the beauty of the Atlantic Ocean and the wildlife that lived in the area.

Florida in the 1500s was alive with loons, mallards, and teals; bald eagles and brown pelicans; Key deer and alligators; and—most magnificent of all—the Florida panther. Lizards, crabs, and sea turtles scurried across endless sands, while parrots and songbirds sang late into the night in the lush evergreen forests that crept slowly toward the sea.

Today's Southeast is quite a bit different from what colonists in the mid-1500s discovered. Yet the area of Virginia, North Carolina, South Carolina, Georgia, and Florida still bears some resemblance to its past. It has the same environments, or biomes, ranging from the coastal wetlands of the southern Atlantic seaboard to the grasslands and pines of the inland regions. It also has the same climate—hot and humid for months out of the year!

One thing the southeastern states no longer share with their past is the quality of their environment. In 1565, as Europe was reeling under the weight of generations of environmental abuse, the American Southeast was still a marvel of ecological balance. When Spanish colonists landed in the New World at the present-day site of St. Augustine, they found a pristine

(opposite page)
Much of the Southeast is blessed by stately palm trees and beautiful sunsets.

wilderness inhabited by peaceful groups of American Indians descended from what are now Asiatic peoples. They also discovered a delicately balanced environmental web in which all of nature was interrelated.

But within the short span of 350 years, the southeastern United States has changed dramatically. Numerous species of plants and animals have disappeared. Streams and rivers run thick with sludge and chemical waste. Wetlands have vanished. Forests have disappeared. Even the air is tainted with carcinogenic poisons.

Some environmentalists say the Southeast will never be the same. Some say it is doomed to destruction.

Once the domain of sawgrass and sand crabs, the Southeast's fragile coastal environment is being destroyed by commercial development.

(opposite page)
Flamingos once roamed wild throughout the Southeast. But a changing environment has caused a reduction in their numbers.

CHAPTER ONE

THE LAND WE WALK

Most of the wildlife in the Southeast lives and thrives in the rich areas of the wetlands. That's where life got its start—not by fighting the surf and fury of the mighty oceans but by moving gradually from the shallow rivers, estuaries, and streams onto the land. These wetlands contained all the necessary ingredients for life—nutrients, moisture, light, and protection from predators.

Fossil records of early life in the United States show that some of the most remarkable creatures on Earth evolved in freshwater swamps and marshes. Some of the largest land animals that ever lived—the sauropod dinosaurs—obtained much of their food from rich ancient wetlands. Their modern-day counterparts—crocodiles and alligators—reach some of their greatest sizes in the wetlands.[1]

Today's salt marshes also produce some of the healthiest plant growth on Earth—growth four times greater than that of modern cornfields. And two thirds of the world's major commercial saltwater fish depend on coastal wetlands at some point in their lives.

At one time, the wetlands were so rich a food source that early colonists plowed lobsters into the soil as fertilizer. Soon, the marshes, glades, and swamps were being diked and drained to provide suitable conditions for growing food crops such as rice and corn. Wetlands, the colonists reasoned, provided poor grazing for cattle and even poorer land for homesteads. They produced swarms of hungry mosquitoes and flooded regularly.

Before long, the Southeast's wetlands were disappearing at a staggering rate. Although a few large tracts of wetlands still

(opposite page)
Pampas grass provides both food and shelter for numerous species of southeastern wildlife.

exist along the eastern shore of Virginia and the Georgia coast, the more heavily populated coastal areas of the Carolinas and Florida have exhausted many of their wetlands. With them have gone the plants, fish, birds, and animals that once made them their home.

THE DELICATE FOOD CHAIN

The wetlands play an important role in the well-being of much of the Southeast's wildlife. Cordgrass in the marshes of central Florida provide food for young crayfish and other crustaceans. The crustaceans provide food for fingerling fish. The fish provide food for woodstorks.

But this interconnected chain is easily broken. When developers cut the cordgrass in order to create a housing development, the crustaceans disappear. After them, the marsh population of fish decreases. The storks, no longer able to feed on the fish, fly farther and farther from their nesting sites to locate food. Young storks still in the nest die from starvation. Even the panthers that prey on a wide variety of wildlife feel the pressures of diminished habitat and move deeper into the wilds—or are struck and killed by trucks and automobiles speeding down the highway.

Today, according to ornithologists—scientists who specialize in the study of birds—as many as 90 percent of all roosting birds have disappeared from the Florida Everglades, the largest freshwater wetland in the continental United States. If something isn't done soon, many of the species that once inhabited the Everglades may soon perish from the Earth.[2]

(opposite page)
Commercial logging operations have destroyed hundreds of thousands of acres of southeastern wildlife habitat.

LOGGING AND WILDLIFE

Throughout the Southeast, where massive commercial logging operations have destroyed most of the old-growth forests (those forests standing since the colonization of America), numerous animal species are in serious danger of extinction. Both the ivory-billed and red-cockaded woodpeckers depend on old-growth forests for survival. The red-cockaded woodpeckers nest in holes drilled in pines at least 80 years old—old enough to contain a certain variety of fungus that weakens the

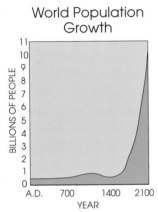

World Population Growth

World population growth and global development are two of the main problems facing the environment.

Sources: Population data from Population Reference Bureau, various publications; historical data from Richard D. Lamm, *Hard Choices* (Denver, CO: May 1985), p. 34

trees' heartwood sufficiently for the woodpeckers to drill. Colonies of two to nine birds may use the same nesting sites for up to 50 years.

But red-cockaded woodpeckers don't play a major role in the Southeast's forestry practices. Since pines grow fastest during the first 20 to 40 years of their life, logging companies reap the greatest profits by cutting them down during that period. As a result, suitable red-cockaded habitat has diminished steadily throughout this century. By 1970, the species was on the endangered list. A 1976 study showed that it was declining in numbers by as much as 13 percent a year.[3] And ivory-billed woodpeckers may already be extinct.

In an effort to save the remaining red-cockaded woodpeckers, the federal government has prepared national guidelines for forests and wildlife refuges throughout the Southeast. These include the exclusion of logging activities within one square mile of existing nesting colonies of woodpeckers.

Unfortunately, not all southeastern animal species are able to survive in such small pockets of forestlands. A Florida panther requires more than 100 square miles of habitat to thrive. Since a healthy breeding population of panthers includes several males and females, suitable habitat must comprise thousands of square miles in order to allow free movement after game such as Key deer.

Once scattered widely throughout the swamplands of the Southeast, today the Florida panther continues to drop in numbers with the increase in commercial logging and residential developments. The current Florida panther population now numbers fewer than 30 animals.[4]

Meanwhile, developers continue draining swamps and converting wetlands into commercial developments. To make matters worse, people often shoot panthers out of ignorance and fear, even though the eastern subspecies has been on state and federal endangered lists since 1968.

THE TOXIC-WASTE PROBLEM

Commercial exploitation isn't the only way in which we're destroying the environment. Today, the Southeast faces a problem of overwhelming proportion—the disposal of toxic

wastes. These wastes come from such substances as industrial chemicals, pesticides, heavy metals, and even common household cleaning products.

Real estate development is destroying the Southeast's marshlands at a staggering rate.

Of the Environmental Protection Agency's (EPA's) National Priorities List of 952 toxic-waste sites in the United States, Florida has three in the top 50—in Pensacola, Tampa, and Plant City. Altogether, southeastern sites total 122—51 in Florida, 7 in Georgia, 21 each in South and North Carolina, and 22 in Virginia.[5]

The problem of toxic wastes is so widespread that the Council on Economic Priorities estimates that eight out of ten Americans live near a hazardous-waste site. The Center for Disease Control recently reported that, in 1980, nearly half of all U.S. residents lived in counties containing a site classified by the EPA as among the most dangerous in the country.

THE WORLD'S MOST HAZARDOUS LANDFILL

The town of Emelle, Alabama, hosts what may well be the world's largest toxic-waste landfill. The site is owned and operated by Chemical Waste Management, Inc. Over the past decade, ChemWaste has been fined more than $25 million for waste-disposal violations. So extensive is the company's list of crimes against the environment, the EPA has set up a special task force to handle them.

But the EPA has been relatively ineffective in dealing with ChemWaste's problems. In fact, several past EPA officials have recently moved to more lucrative positions on ChemWaste's staff. "The collusion between industry and its regulator is now so close," according to the article, "that EPA toxic-waste administrator Hugh Kaufman once complained, 'Sometimes the EPA acts as if it were a wholly owned subsidiary of ChemWaste Management.'"

The Emelle landfill was only two years old when Alabama governor George Wallace's son-in-law bought some land, obtained the necessary operating permits with surprising ease, and immediately sold the land to ChemWaste. His profit from the deal was estimated at $15 million to $30 million.

Today, various government programs are under way to clean up the Southeast's toxic-waste sites. North Carolina alone has 60 such programs. Its "Pollution Prevention Pays" program, for example, costs taxpayers approximately $650,000 a year, much of it going to provide on-site technical assistance. In return, the state's environmental programs saved an estimated $16 million in 1987 alone.[6]

HEAVY METALS AND HUMAN HEALTH

Heavy metals, too, play a role in creating hazardous waste, and they often come from seemingly innocent sources.

Dead car batteries have created headaches for anxious motorists for years. Now, they're creating hazardous waste. Discarded batteries are accumulating behind gas stations and in landfills at a staggering rate, increasing the possibility of groundwater contamination from lead, an extremely toxic metal. Many southeastern municipalities and most rural residents get their drinking water from groundwater supplies.

(opposite page)
Although these toxic wastes are sealed in steel drums, their permanent disposal remains a critical environmental problem.

17

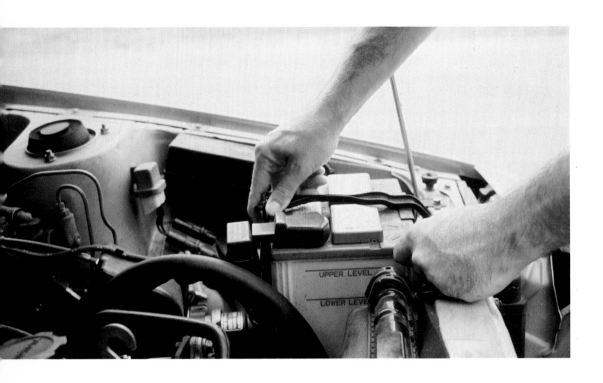

Each year, nearly 80 million lead-acid batteries die on U.S. motorists. Up to 3 billion pounds of them are dumped annually. Service stations that once paid $3 apiece in order to recycle dead batteries now take them, as one dealer admitted, "only as a courtesy." Recycling rates for lead-acid batteries have dropped from 76 percent in 1974 to 58 percent in 1985. One reason for this drop is an overabundance of lead in the marketplace, making the recycling of lead economically unattractive. Another reason is the hazard of handling the metal. Lead has been proved to cause anemia, anorexia, nerve damage, paralysis, and even death.

As a result of stockpiling batteries, lead and other heavy metals have been discovered in soil and stream sediments around the Palmetto Recycling plant in Columbia, South Carolina. To make matters worse, car batteries are only part of the problem. Each year, about 1 billion household batteries are manufactured for flashlights, toys, and radios. Most of them wind up in municipal landfills where they can leach lead, zinc, and other toxic substances down through the soil.

Each year, nearly 3 billion pounds of toxic batteries are disposed of in the United States.

NUCLEAR WASTES

Nuclear wastes pose a special problem. Although nuclear fission reactors have only been in existence since World War II, they have generated large amounts of waste—most in the form of spent radioactive fuel rods that still contain substantial amounts of radioactivity.

The main problem with disposing of nuclear waste is its extremely long life. Some estimates indicate that high-level radioactive wastes may remain contaminated for half a million years, which is longer by far than humankind has existed! Finding a way to store these wastes safely is difficult. Current plans to locate a permanent underground storage site have run into difficulties. In the meantime, nuclear wastes are being stored temporarily at those sites generating them.

Even low-level radioactive wastes—medical fluids, power reactor fluids, contaminated employee clothing, and plastics that remain hazardous for up to 300 years—present serious disposal problems. In the past, these wastes have been buried at various commercial sites. But one such site located near Barnwell, South Carolina, was recently closed for safety reasons. Another in Aiken, South Carolina, is targeted by environmentalists as one of the worst polluters in the nation.

NUCLEAR ACCIDENTS

Nuclear accidents are another major hazard facing the Southeast. In 1987, numerous nuclear reactors were cited by the Public Citizen's *Nuclear Power Safety Report* for having an excessively high number of "licensee event reports" (LERs). LERs range from relatively minor nuclear-plant incidents to near-catastrophes.

Although the nationwide nuclear industry average for LERs is 27 a year, one plant in Waynesboro, Georgia, had 75. The Shearon Harris-1 reactor in New Hill, North Carolina, had 62, and the Catawba-1 in Clover, South Carolina, had 44.[7]

These LERs are serious indicators of mismanagement or technical flaws in buildings or equipment. But they seem like little more than minor annoyances compared with the continuing string of accidents and near-catastrophes at the Savannah

River nuclear weapons production facility in Aiken, South Carolina, according to a recent congressional subcommittee investigating the facility.

The Savannah River facility is run under federal contract by DuPont, which is responsible for maintaining safe reactor operations. But this form of self-regulation has resulted in serious problems over the years, many of which had been kept secret from the public until recently.

A 1985 memo by DuPont scientist G. C. Ridgely, made public for the first time at an October 1988 hearing before the House Government Operations Subcommittee on Environment, Energy and Natural Resources (SYNAR), summarized some of the worst of Savannah River's incidents.

- A 1957 test caused the melting of a nuclear fuel assembly.

- A 1960 nuclear reactor start-up caused power to surge at 12 times the normal rate of 500 megawatts per minute. The reactor was 40 seconds from having the core coolant boil.

- A 1965 leak into an airduct deposited so much plutonium that the duct almost went "critical"—a term used by the industry to describe a major nuclear reactor accident.

- A 1970 melting of a nuclear fuel rod caused a significant release of radiation into the plant, resulting in a 900-person, 3-month cleanup.[8]

(opposite page)
South Carolina's Savannah River nuclear weapons facility is one of the most dangerous in the nation.

- An accident in 1982 leaked plutonium-contaminated water for 12 hours.

- An average of 9 to 12 forced shutdowns a year have taken place over the last 17 years.

Richard Starostecki, senior Department of Energy (DOE) deputy assistant secretary for safety, health, and quality assurance, said after the hearing, "There are currently some senior managers within the department [who have] an attitude toward production reactor safety which on the face seems to be similar to that which existed in the space program prior to the *Challenger* accident."

In fact, an investigation by the U.S. General Accounting Office discovered radioactive materials in the groundwater near the plant at more than 400 times the proposed drinking water standard. Although some of the radiation may have

seeped gradually into the water table during the 1950s and 1960s, when DOE regularly dumped low-level nuclear wastes into shallow ponds and burial pits, much of it comes from accidental discharges.

In 1987 alone, U.S. nuclear plants recorded nearly 3,000 mishaps and an amazing 765 emergency shutdowns. At least 18 of these shutdowns came as a result of serious accidents that could have led to extended core damage and nuclear disaster.

Of the world's 400 nuclear reactors, 108 are situated in the United States. Of these, 22 are scattered throughout the Southeast, including 5 in Florida, 5 in North Carolina, 4 in South Carolina, 4 in Georgia, and 4 in Virginia.[9]

Recycled plastic bottles can be made into numerous products ranging from building blocks to synthetic carpets.

NEW HOPE FOR OLD TRASH

Besides toxic and nuclear waste, the Southeast is currently deluged by tons of solid waste—the everyday trash coming from businesses and households throughout the region. As landfills

continue to operate beyond capacity, new, safe means of disposing of trash are being sought. One of the least expensive and most promising is recycling—the process of turning used materials into new products.

The United States currently recycles about 11 percent of its solid waste, burns some 6 percent, and places the rest in landfills—a whopping 83 percent. Japan, on the other hand, recycles more than 50 percent and landfills only 27 percent.[10]

Yet Americans can be extremely inventive, as a few people in Summerville, Georgia, have been demonstrating.

Image Carpets currently manufactures a line of synthetic carpets for home and office. The carpets are made from recycled plastic soda bottles. It takes about 50 bottles to produce one square yard of carpet from the recycled plastic. Image Carpets currently employs about 900 persons. If the recycling process works as expected, the company and others like it will grow even larger. Using discarded plastic bottles is cheaper than using newly produced polyester. According to Kelly Hudson, president of Image Carpets, the new, recycled carpet is just as durable, stain-resistant, and attractive as carpet produced from new polyester.

Image Carpets still faces one minor problem. It needs more bottles for its carpets. But there's no shortage of them at the nation's dumps. It's just a matter of collecting and recycling them before they turn into environmentally polluting waste.

Part of the reason for the low U. S. recycling rate is a lack of mandatory recycling programs. Although various voluntary programs in cities such as Atlanta, Tampa, Miami, Charlotte, and Richmond are promising, they're simply not enough.

CHAPTER TWO

THE AIR WE BREATHE

Breathe in. Stop. Wait. In less time than it takes to watch a 30-second television commercial, you have just bathed your lungs in pollution. Inside air, outside air—it doesn't matter.

And if you happen to live in a major metropolitan area such as Miami, Tampa, Augusta, Charlotte, Birmingham, or Montgomery, the air you breathe in every few seconds is probably loaded with toxic chemicals. In fact, if the air you breathe were tested by the EPA, it would probably fail federal clean-air standards.

A 1989 EPA survey of industrial air pollution reported an estimated 2.4 *billion* pounds of chemicals in the nation's air in 1987. These chemicals are capable of causing cancer, neurological disease, or birth defects. More than one third come from the chemical industry. Most of the rest come from paper, metal, plastic, rubber, electrical equipment, petroleum, and furniture manufacturing.

The actual totals of pollutants were probably much higher, though, because the EPA survey failed to include such sources as automobile exhausts, toxic-waste dumps, and companies emitting fewer than 75,000 pounds of toxins into the air each year.[1]

Although the greatest concentration of cancer-causing pollutants occurs in the Northeast, seven sites were found in North Carolina; three in South Carolina; three in Virginia; seven in Georgia; and eight in Florida.

Most of this pollution consists of sulfur dioxide, which, when mixed with water vapor in the atmosphere, produces sulfuric acid; carbon monoxide (a by-product of burning fossil fuels); nitrogen dioxide (created when fuel is burned at high

(opposite page)
Despite tougher air pollution laws, pollutants continue to flow from the Southeast's industrial smokestacks.

temperatures, as in automobiles); particulates (tiny dust particles created by burning fossil fuels and wood); hydrocarbons such as benzene, methane, and butane (from the incomplete burning of fossil fuels in automobiles and furnaces and from industrial solvents, oil spills, forest fires, and decaying plants); ozone (from lightning, high-voltage equipment, motor vehicles, and industry); and lead (from gasoline, industrial smelting, and the manufacture and disposal of batteries).[2]

ALL SMOGGED IN

Smog (mostly ozone and peroxyacetyl nitrate—PAN) is created when sunlight "cooks" various emissions from sources such as industrial smokestacks and automobile exhausts. Other sources include house paints and the gasoline vapors that escape when cars and underground gasoline station tanks are being filled.

Although Los Angeles has long been the U.S. leader in the production of ozone smog (registering more than 176 days of excessive ozone in 1988), it's hardly alone. A recent EPA report on unsafe ozone levels in a large number of cities throughout the country included Atlanta, Georgia; Miami, Tampa, Jacksonville, St. Petersburg, and Clearwater, Florida; Norfolk, Virginia Beach, and Newport News, Virginia; Columbia, Greenville, and Spartanburg, South Carolina; and Fayetteville, Charlotte, Gastonia, Rock Hill, Greensboro, Winston-Salem, and High Point, North Carolina.[3]

What's worse, ozone smog levels are increasing despite various vehicle-emission controls placed on motor vehicles during the last 20 years. One of the main reasons is that automobile use rose by 25 percent between 1977 and 1988. Truck use rose by 40 percent during the same period.

The result is more smog, particularly in urban areas where motor-vehicle use is greatest. But there has recently been an alarming increase in smog in rural areas, and that has environmentalists worried.

At Shenandoah National Park in Virginia's Blue Ridge Mountains, former superintendent Bob Jacobson sits looking out over the valley below. What he sees are 10 to 14 miles of some of the most beautiful scenery in the Southeast. That's a

far cry from what he used to see. When the park was created half a century ago, visitors looking east could catch a glimpse of the Washington Monument 70 miles away.

"There are some times now when 5 miles might be the absolute maximum visibility," Jacobson says. That means the Shenandoah River, which is less than 10 miles away, is hidden from view by smog.

The problem, according to scientists, is sulfate haze—a thick layer of smog created by sulfur dioxide emissions reacting with sunlight in the atmosphere. The sulfur dioxide, which comes from the burning of fossil fuels, is a main ingredient in the phenomenon known as acid rain.

Vehicle exhausts are among the main sources of ozone and urban smog.

Problems such as those in Shenandoah National Park are mainly a result of attempts by major cities—some more than 1,000 miles away—to clean up their air. Industries and utilities erected towering smokestacks in the 1970s that sent emissions high into the atmosphere. Instead of settling over those cities such as Birmingham, Atlanta, and Miami, where the pollutants originated, the smog drifted north and northeast on prevailing winds.[4]

The EPA confirms what people such as Jacobson already know—that average visibility has declined throughout some areas of the Southeast from more than 55 miles to under 12 miles in less than a century. Air-quality experts say the problem is likely to get worse before it gets better as increased sulfur emissions from the use of cheap, abundant coal are expected to rise.

Ozone pollution is also a serious human health problem for the residents of many U.S. cities. In most cities, the number of hospital admissions for asthma, bronchitis, and pneumonia rises with increased ozone levels.[5] Problems range from difficulty in breathing to burning eyes, headaches, and nausea. In addition, research by the American Lung Association indicates that long-term exposure to high ozone levels can increase the aging of human lungs and decrease the effectiveness of the body's immune system.

Ozone pollution also makes many crops less resistant to insects. Such typical southeastern crops as corn, tobacco, peanuts, and soybeans may suffer losses totaling more than $2 billion each year.[6]

Ozone may also be damaging to southeastern forests. Recent studies suggest that the dying of forests at high elevations in parks such as Virginia's Shenandoah may be due in part from high ozone levels.

ACID RAIN

Until recently, acid rain—produced by burning fossil fuels in power plants, industry, and motor vehicles—had been thought to be a problem confined to the North Central and Northeast states. But when pollutants such as nitrogen oxides and sulfur combine with moisture in the atmosphere to create sulfuric and nitric acids, they often drift southeast on prevailing winds. The results, according to recent studies on the effects of acid rain in the Southeast, are frightening. Virtually all water samples taken from the five southeastern states showed signs of acidification. Over half the lakes in northern Florida are highly acidified.

The problem with acidified waterways is that, as the acidity increases, aquatic life decreases. Most healthy lakes measure about 7.0 on a pH scale—a scale of measurement to determine the amount of acidity or alkalinity in a liquid. On the scale, the number 14 represents the highest possible alkalinity (lye has a pH of 13). The number 7 is neutral (as with distilled water). And the number 0 represents the highest possible acidity (battery acid has a pH of 1). At pH 6.0, most trout, clams, and crustaceans show serious signs of decline. At pH 5.5, rainbow and brown trout begin to die; brook trout fail to reproduce; and many clams and crustaceans die. At pH 5.0, most species experience difficulty in reproducing. At pH 4.2, the common toad dies. At pH 3.5, nearly all fish, clams, snails, and frogs die. At pH 2.5, only a few species of midges, fungi, and bacteria can survive.

Acid rain also affects human beings. As highly toxic acids concentrate in the air, particularly in urban areas, people with bronchial problems such as asthma and bronchitis experience increased respiratory problems. Although further studies need to be conducted, preliminary tests run in Atlanta indicate a significant relationship between the number of people entering Atlanta hospitals and the amount of acidity in the city's air.

In addition, acid rain takes its toll economically. In 1987, acidic precipitation ate away the paint on 2,000 luxury BMWs that had just arrived in Jacksonville, Florida, from West Germany. As a result, BMW moved its point-of-entry out of the city, costing Jacksonville hundreds of thousands of dollars in jobs each year.

Environmentalists insist that acid rain is controllable through tougher industrial and auto-emissions laws. But little has been done to stop the problem. As a result, the Southeast continues to suffer. Of the 20 most acidic rain samples collected in the United States in 1987, one was from Florida and three were from North Carolina.

THE WATER
WE DRINK

This planet composed of three-quarters water plays host to a society of walking, talking, and thinking mammals called human beings. Like all land animals, human beings are thought to have originated in the seas. As they evolved from swimming organisms into land mammals, they developed the abilities that have separated them from the rest of the animal kingdom.

But before human beings inhabited the Earth, another group of mammals with highly developed brains had emerged from the seas. These mammals roamed the land on four legs—not two. Their bodies were covered with hair for protection from the elements. As time passed, these mammals had difficulty finding food on land and gradually returned to the sea, where food was plentiful.

Over time, these ocean-going mammals lost their hair and evolved a flat, powerful tail to propel themselves through the water. They developed sonar to locate food and detect the presence of their enemies. They grew to depend upon one another for security. These highly developed animals are called dolphins—humankind's closest sea-dwelling relatives.

Ever since the waters of the world gave birth to life, the dolphins have played a critical role in the environment. Yet today, they are in trouble. They're hunted for food, trapped by tuna nets and drowned at sea, killed by toxic chemicals washed into the oceans, destroyed by poisonous heavy metals and toxic wastes accumulating in their food supplies. And the dolphins aren't alone.

Countless southeastern lakes, rivers, ponds, and streams are being threatened by pollution. The pollutants take many

(opposite page)
Once, all water was pure and clean. Today, even the sprawling oceans are showing the strains of pollution.

forms—chemical runoff, oil and gasoline spills, solid waste from urban developments, toxic wastes leached from landfills, acid rain from industrial smokestacks, and so on. Even the mighty Atlantic Ocean has become a huge sink for the disposal of garbage and other wastes. Still, the pollution continues. Nowhere is the problem of water pollution so apparent as in America's wetlands.

Toxic Substances Discharged by U.S. Industry, 1987

Destination	Millions of Pounds
Air	2700
Lakes, Rivers and Streams	550
Landfills and Earthen Pits	3900
Treatment and Disposal Facilities	3300
Total	10450

Source: Environmental Protection Agency, reported in *The Washington Post*, April 13, 1989, p. A33

WETLANDS AND WATER PURIFICATION

Wetlands play an important role in replenishing groundwater and in acting as a natural water purifier. Wetland plants can absorb excess nutrients and can help to immobilize pesticides, heavy metals, and other toxins, preventing them from moving up the food chain. Wetlands in Florida have even been used to treat sewage successfully for years.

But the United States has already lost half of its wetlands to urban and agricultural development. The current annual loss is estimated at 450,000 acres, an area half the size of the state of Rhode Island.

The Florida Everglades, among the world's largest freshwater wetland areas, has played an important role in maintaining the balance of nature for millions of years. But it, too, is in trouble. The Everglades, which is actually a river more than 50 miles wide and a few inches deep, flows slowly over a riverbed that drops only a few feet in elevation for more than 100 miles.

Over thousands of years, plants and animals have adapted to the natural rise and fall of water in the Everglades. Broad sawgrass prairies; giant stands of mangrove, cypress, and hardwood trees; freshwater sloughs; and coastal marshes all distinguish this from other wilderness areas in the United States.

(opposite page)
The Florida alligator, once hunted to near extinction, today faces an even more frightening challenge–dwindling marshlands.

Life in the Everglades has always been fragile. Only a few inches of soil cover the limestone formations that hold the groundwater. As long as the water continues to flow through the wetlands in a natural cycle of wet summers and dry winters, the Everglades teem with life.

But something has happened recently to change that cycle. At Florida's Loxahatchee Wildlife Refuge, the alligators are

leaving and crawling along highways, into farmers' fields, and right up to houses. The reason? Three hundred thousand new people move to Florida each year. As people move in, the wilderness disappears. And the food for such predators as the Florida alligator grows more and more scarce.

The largest wetland in the United States begins at Lake Okeechobee. This sprawling inland lake once poured an endless stream of fresh water into the Florida Everglades to the south. Today, that water is contaminated with residential waste and agricultural runoff—and worse.

The Everglades is being swallowed up in huge chunks. People desperate to return to nature are moving into residential developments in record numbers. Dairy farmers anxious to escape the hardships of life in the North are buying thousands of acres of newly created Florida farmland. Meanwhile, wildlife in the Everglades is forced to look elsewhere for food and shelter.[1]

"Without a major change in public policy," according to Michael Finley, former superintendent of Everglades National Park, "this will surely die. We're looking at a lake writhing in pain in the last stages of its life."

The Everglades' problems started in the early 1960s. That's when the state and the Army Corps of Engineers turned the 100-mile-long scenic, meandering Kissimmee River into a 53-mile straight drainage canal to prevent flooding and create agricultural land.

Channeling the Kissimmee changed marshes and swamps into highly productive farms. People who had opposed the $31 million project were furious, according to John Jones, author of a 1976 plan to restore the Kissimmee to its original state. "It wasn't done for flood control," according to Jones. "It was done for profit."

Meanwhile, billions of gallons of precious water—water that once supported the fragile Everglades' ecosystem—were being diverted to pumps used to irrigate sugarcane plantations. Billions more were being siphoned off for the swimming pools of Miami and Palm Beach. This gradual loss of precious water has caused a dramatic shift in the Everglades' native habitat from sawgrass and wet prairies to solid stands of cattails that are slowly choking the remaining lakes, ponds, and sloughs to death. That and the most severe drought in recent history have left the Everglades reeling.

As the natural habitat continues to change, the food chain gradually grows shorter. The alligators are so hungry they're literally jumping into boats and stealing bait from fishermen. Such species as the woodstork, snail kite, and Florida panther are already seriously endangered.

Once, the Kissimmee River was the anchor for the 700-square-mile ecosystem stretching from the river south through Lake Okeechobee and down into the Everglades. The river's curves and bends acted as a sort of natural filtration system, removing many of the pollutants from the water before they could reach the fragile breeding grounds of the Everglades. Now, all that is gone.

From the time the Army Corps of Engineers opened the first lock on the river, the environment began to change. Forty-five thousand acres of wetlands were wiped out nearly overnight. Six species of fish were obliterated. Countless wading birds disappeared. Millions of gallons of polluted water began flowing into Lake Okeechobee. From there, they were funneled into the Everglades, where state biologists recently found the first signs of toxic mercury poisoning in Florida fish in history.

ENDANGERED FLORIDA WILDLIFE

Other species of Everglades wildlife are suffering, too. Nearly 400 endangered species totter on the brink of extinction, more than in any other area of the continental United States. "Environmentalists now predict that many of the endangered species that are surviving in Florida may become extinct within our lifetime," according to David Hitzig of the Audubon Society.

Only 30 or fewer Florida panthers and fewer than 1,000 manatees live here. The burrowing owl and gopher tortoise are also on their way to extinction, as is the woodstork, the only stork native to North America. In 1935, more than 150,000 breeding pairs of wading birds lived in the Everglades. In 1990, only 375 nests were found, and many of them were abandoned because of a lack of food and shortage of water.

The number of nesting shorebirds in Florida's Everglades is declining at a frightening pace.

"When we obliterate large areas of natural habitat," says Mark Robson of the Florida Fresh Water Fish and Game Commission, "most of the wildlife simply can't reproduce and survive any longer."

Slowly, the prairies, sloughs, and sawgrass marshes of the Everglades are being replaced by weeds growing in a flood of organic waste. "Birds don't feed in it, animals don't move in it, and fish can't live in it because there's no oxygen," according to Paul Parks of the Florida Wildlife Federation. "It's just biological trash, really."

At the present time, the life expectancy of Everglades National Park is only five to ten more years, according to John Ogden, wildlife researcher. "At that point, it will be too late to save."

RESTORING THE EVERGLADES

While we can never hope to return the Everglades to its original state, we must do everything in our power to take the first critical steps—to stop the pollution, to extend the park's lifetime, and to halt the onslaught of human abuse. And that's exactly what the state's current governor hopes to do.

The governor of Florida, Bob Martinez, hopes to raise $3 billion within the next several years to buy up and buy back environmentally sensitive lands in an effort to restore the Everglades. The program would be the most ambitious ever undertaken. It would start by returning the Kissimmee to its original state.

But the restoration will not be cheap. Current estimates put the cost of backfilling the canal and restoring the Kissimmee to its original state at more than $270 million. Tens of millions of dollars more will be required to clean up Lake Okeechobee and move adjacent dairy farms to new sites away from the waterway. An additional $90 million will be needed to purchase the environmentally sensitive lands to discourage future development.

The plan has its share of skeptics. Among them is John Jones, who wrote the original Kissimmee Restoration Act more than a decade ago. Jones doubts the governor's ability to seize the land back from the special-interest groups that stand to lose a substantial amount of money if the restoration plan goes through.

"The South Florida Water Management District is dragging its feet," says Jones. "They're being influenced by people such as cattlemen, dairymen, farmers, real estate people . . . who have vested interests [in the river]."

ACID RAIN AND WATER POLLUTION

Acid rain caused by industrial pollution has been known since 1872 when Robert Angus Smith discussed its appearance in England following the Industrial Revolution. It wasn't until 1961, though, that the problem began to be taken seriously when Swedish scientist Svante Oden discovered evidence of acid rain in Scandinavia. He took his findings to the press instead of to the scientific journals. More recently, acid rain has been pegged as one of the most persistent, widespread sources of air, land, and water pollution known.

According to a recent study based on data gathered by a national conservation organization, half the streams in the mid-Atlantic and southeastern states—areas not normally associated with acid rain—are either highly acidic or on the verge of becoming so. In addition, several studies have shown that acid rain is not only on the increase throughout the Southeast, but its effects are more varied than originally thought. Besides acidifying the region's waterways, acid rain—high in both sulfur oxides and nitrogen—is now suspected of increasing the nitrogen level in various southeastern lakes and streams. Higher nitrogen levels result in increased algae growth, which leads to eutrophication, or the depletion of oxygen.

As much as 25 percent of the nitrogen content in several southeastern waterways, including the Everglades, is now thought to come from the nitrogen content in acid rain. Prior to the studies, agricultural runoff and sewage discharges had been blamed entirely for the problem.

Besides losing its lakes, rivers, streams, and wetlands, the southeastern states are finding their groundwater supplies affected by acid rain. The reason is that acidity has the ability to leach unwanted substances into fresh-water supplies. As the acidity of water increases, numerous heavy metals, including toxic aluminum, cadmium, copper, mercury, and lead, are released into the water. These metals are known to cause a wide variety of serious diseases—from kidney damage and cancer to Alzheimer's and Parkinson's diseases.

The problem of acidic water and leaching is especially critical in the Southeast. There the soil is naturally thin, sandy, and already slightly acidic, and groundwater tables are relatively close to the Earth's surface.

RED TIDES

As sewage and agricultural runoff flow into the Atlantic Ocean, large quantities of nitrogen and phosphorus pollute the water. These compounds nourish various algae species and

cause an explosive growth called an algal bloom, or red tide. The algae turn the water green, brown, yellow, or red, depending on the species involved.

Explosive growths of algae, called red tides, are toxic to marine life.

As the carpet of algae grows denser, it blocks off all sunlight and consumes the nutrients in the water. Eventually, the algae begin to die. Their decaying bodies deplete the water of dissolved oxygen, suffocating other forms of aquatic life nearby. One such massive die-off, called a "dead zone," that occurred off the coast of Florida in the Gulf of Mexico measured more than 3,000 square miles!

Some types of algae can also be toxic to marine life. In 1987, thousands of mullet and nearly the entire population of scallops were wiped out off the Carolina coast due to toxins from an algal bloom. What's worse, toxic algae can work their way up the food chain, causing even more destruction. A study by the National Oceanic and Atmospheric Administration concluded that, between 1987 and 1989, as many as 3,000 dolphins in the area may have died after eating fish contaminated with toxic algae.[2]

TOXIC CHEMICALS

Toxic chemicals enter the bays and oceans of the southeastern United States daily. At Hopewell, Virginia, the toxic chlorinated hydrocarbon Kepone had been dumped into the James River for more than a decade. The chemical was widely used throughout the South to control fire ants. Although the dumping stopped in the mid-1970s, the chemical is still poisoning marine life downstream.

At the U.S. naval base at Norfolk, Virginia, a biocide used to protect the hulls of ships is proving deadly to marine life. Tributyl tin (TBT) is far more toxic and longer-lasting than copper-based paints. Even low concentrations have toxic effects on oyster and clam larvae. TBT can also accumulate in the food chain and become harmful to human beings. Yet nearly 50 percent of all recreational boats in the Chesapeake Bay, as well as many larger commercial and military ships, regularly use TBT. Although the EPA has promised to consider restricting the use of TBT to deep-water vessels, the agency has yet to act.[3]

OFFSHORE OIL

One of the most serious threats to the Southeast's environment is offshore oil. As productive inland drilling sites have grown increasingly scarce, the oil industry has turned toward new, more promising drilling sites. These include a number of sites located off Louisiana and Texas in the western Gulf of Mexico. The oil industry, concentrating its offshore drilling efforts in the Gulf of Mexico, hadn't gotten around to considering significant drilling off the environmentally sensitive coastal lands of Florida—at least not until recently.

(opposite page)
Anti-fouling paint on the hulls of boats and ships poses a serious threat to the marine environment.

In 1973, Exxon invested $200 million on an offshore lease in the Destin Dome off the Florida panhandle, only to come up with a dry hole. Other oil companies sank several exploratory, or wildcat, wells at various locations along Florida's coast, including Florida Bay and the Keys during the 1940s and mid-1950s. None of the wells proved successful.

Today, new technological advances have rekindled the interest of several major oil companies now anxious to obtain leas-

es for the South Florida Basin. This basin is one of the last great untapped reserves of oil in the United States. "That's about 15 million acres without a well in it," according to Jack W. Schanck, regional exploration manager for Unocal Corp, a major oil-production company. "That's a pretty rare entity in the continental U.S. at this point in time." The Florida land compares in size to an area in offshore Louisiana where up to 4,000 exploratory wells have been punched into the seabed.

The region of Florida showing the most promise, according to geologists, consists of about 1,000 blocks of leased land. Each block consists of 5,760 acres located in federally controlled waters from Naples, Florida, in the north to a point off the middle Keys in the south. Several oil companies have already paid the government about $100 million for 70 leases in the area known as Pulley Ridge. Believing this area shows enough promise to merit investing the $6 million to $7 million required to sink a wildcat well, Unocal and Mobil have asked the federal government for permission to drill.

But Florida residents, environmentalists, and politicians don't want the companies to drill. They're concerned that an accident might spill oil into the sea. From there, it would quickly travel down and around the Keys and through the Florida Straits, coating miles of sensitive shrimp and fish hatcheries, reefs, and mangrove stands.

"A spill would go around the Tortugas and up the Keys like a freight train," according to Paul G. Johnson, a senior analyst with the Florida state governor's Office of Environmental Affairs. "If the very essence of South Florida living is related to those natural resources, why jeopardize them to a 30-year boom to bust?" Johnson asks, referring to the average life span of a producing well.

At the federal level, Florida members of Congress have successfully argued for a temporary moratorium, or halt, on all drilling while the projects are studied. Meanwhile, some state representatives are proposing a bill that would make the moratorium permanent. That would require the government to buy back the leases from the oil companies. The success of such a bill, though, is uncertain, since it will have to go through congressional committees that include several members anxious to see the oil companies prosper.

ESTABLISHING MORE RESTRAINTS

Recognizing that the oil companies will likely get their way, several Florida legislators are proposing to hit the oil producers where it hurts the most—in their pocketbooks. By proposing surcharges on all oil removed from the area and insisting that oil companies maintain all the necessary pollution-control equipment to handle a potential accident, they hope to "put a price tag on it and make it so expensive they [the oil companies] won't want to do it," according to Democratic representative Ron Saunders.

An alternative might require the oil industry to meet stricter safety and anti-pollution regulations. Chevron, one of the largest leaseholders in the Pulley Ridge area, currently operates a zero-discharge oil rig in the Mississippi Sound off the coast of Gulfport. The rig is virtually nonpolluting. All discharges from the drilling process are collected and monitored. A barge tied to a piling collects the debris, which is shipped to shore for proper disposal. Even the rig's toilets are filled with mineral oil so that the waste material will evaporate into a sludge, which can then be removed and taken ashore.

"Nobody is going to spit off of this rig," says Chevron engineer Andy Rawicki. "Our requirement here is that we don't release anything. Period."

Such a rig isn't cheap, even by oil-industry standards. The total cost is expected to reach $22 million, $4 million of which would go toward environmental safety modifications.[4] But this may be an indication that the oil industry can be forced to clean up its act. On the other hand, no one can actually prepare for such extraordinary offshore accidents as explosions, blown well caps, ruptures in the sea floor, and other things that might release hundreds of thousands of barrels into one of the most environmentally sensitive regions on Earth.

Meanwhile, the battle over offshore Florida oil continues—a battle involving profit-driven oil companies on one hand and concerned citizens and environmentalists on the other. The oil companies point to an America starving for fuel. Meanwhile, the environmentalists point to a dismal record of lies, deceit, and pollution by the oil industry in the past and ask simply, "Would you trust your life to these people?"

A TIME FOR ACTION

Throughout the Southeast, the list of endangered animals grows longer each year. On it are the American alligator, gray bat, American crocodile, Okaloosa darter, Key deer, southern bald eagle, Florida snail kite, Florida manatee, Florida panther, red-cockaded woodpecker, eastern cougar, American ivory-billed woodpecker, and many, many more.

In addition, nearly 8 percent of all plant species are endangered, according to the Center for Plant Conservation. Another 700 may become extinct by the year 2000.

During the past 600 million years, the worldwide natural extinction rate has averaged about one species a year. Throughout the world today, that rate is estimated to be one to three species lost each day—perhaps as many as one an hour! Scientists speculate that, by the early 21st century, the worldwide extinction rate may skyrocket to several hundred species a day! At that rate, the world may have just half the species of plants and animals it currently has in just two generations.

Luckily, some people in the Southeast have decided to do something about it.

THE EPA TAKES ACTION

Three hundred years ago, more than 215 million acres of wetlands existed in what is now the continental United States. Today, there are fewer than 99 million acres—or less than half. In an effort to stem the loss of America's most important and fragile environment, the EPA announced in 1987 that it was going to begin taking a more active role in protecting America's wetlands. This role is based on its new powers

(opposite page)
The Florida panther once roamed the entire Southeast. Today, it's headed for extinction.

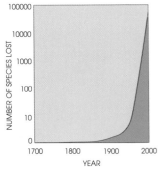

Estimated Annual
Rate of Species
Loss, 1700-2000

Source: Based on estimates in Norman
Myers (ed., *Gaia: An Atlas of Planet
Management* (Garden City, NY:
Anchor Books, 1984), p. 155

(opposite page)
*The peaceful Florida
manatee faces two dis-
tinct dangers–the pro-
pellers from pleasure
boats and toxic
pollution.*

under the Clean Water Act originally enacted in 1977 and updated several times since.

The agency quickly moved against three developers in Illinois, fining them thousands of dollars for illegally filling marshlands. It then rejected a controversial plan to build a recreational area at Lake Alma in southern Georgia. "The project would have wasted tax dollars on an economically questionable venture and would have ruined important wetlands and other habitat in the process," according to National Wildlife Federation president Jay D. Hair, who applauded the decision.

In 1989, the EPA further announced that it would maintain the total number of wetlands in the country at present levels, either by preventing the destruction of existing wetlands or by creating new wetlands to match the size of those destroyed. As a result of agency-conducted studies, the EPA identified polluted wetlands in 49 states. (Although Arizona didn't report, it's presumed to have polluted wetlands as well.) It went on to identify 240 local governments, 627 industrial plants, and 12 federal installations, including several military bases and U.S. Department of Energy nuclear facilities. The agency gave the polluters until June 4, 1992, to stop their polluting, after which time violators will be subject to fines and additional penalties.

The results of the EPA's actions are mixed. Although there's been an overall loss of wildlife habitat throughout the Southeast, there have also been some reasons to celebrate. Attempts to reintroduce the red wolf to the wilderness in North Carolina are showing signs of success; the once-endangered brown pelican is now flourishing, actually extending its range in many coastal areas; and the population of striped bass in the Southeast is growing at a healthy rate.

MEETING NEW GUIDELINES

Currently, more than 12,000 chemical-manufacturing plants, 400,000 major chemical storage facilities, and several million users or storers of potentially dangerous amounts of toxic chemicals are located throughout the United States. Although numerous federal and state regulations govern the use and

handling of a wide range of chemicals, EPA efforts to monitor the safety of these facilities have generally failed.

But one man recently discovered a problem and did something about it. Garland Ross is a senior engineer at Yale Materials Handling Corporation's Lenoir, North Carolina, plant. When he discovered that the plant was emitting 2,000 pounds a year of the highly toxic chemical 1,1,1-trichloroethane, a solvent used to clean and degrease metal cylinders, he was shocked.

Ross set about finding a workable substitute for the chemical, and in early 1988, he discovered a safer, water-based rinse. The plant has been using it ever since. The switch has cut Yale's cleaning costs by almost half. It also no longer adds to the cost of hazardous-waste disposal.[1]

If more toxic-chemical companies discovered that meeting government requirements makes good business sense, the environment throughout the Southeast would soon take a turn for the better. "In many cases," according to Charles L. Elkins, director of the EPA's Office of Toxic Substances, "companies will find that doing so is good business as well as good community relations. The savings from controlling waste and improving process efficiencies often outweigh the costs.

"The question now is whether America's manufacturers will seize the initiative to reduce their toxic emissions voluntarily—or wait for their workers, their communities, or their government to prod them into action."

BENEFICIAL BACTERIA DISCOVERED

Scientists analyzing several test holes drilled at the Savannah River Nuclear Plant in Aiken, South Carolina, recently discovered microorganisms "in great abundance and diversity." The organisms were discovered 850 feet below the Earth's surface—the deepest depth yet probed.

Of the more than 3,000 types of bacteria discovered, only a handful have so far been classified, according to Carl Fliermans, a DuPont microbial ecologist working on the project for the U.S. government. Fliermans expects to discover thousands of additional organisms in new test holes. Some are scheduled to be drilled as deep as 2,000 feet.

Fliermans and other scientists around the world are hopeful about these new species. Some have already shown the ability to produce various antibiotics and to neutralize toxic substances. They may have a bright future in medicine, as well as in the control of toxic waste and pollution.

CONSERVATION GROUPS PITCH IN

Numerous conservation organizations such as the Audubon Society, Citizens for a Better Environment, Ducks Unlimited, and the Nature Conservancy are helping various state and federal agencies stop the destruction of the Southeast's wetlands. These and other agencies have acquired more than 250,000 acres of wetlands along rivers, lakes, and marshes throughout the Southeast. Various private industrial firms and giant corporations have also donated thousands of acres of southern swamplands, such as North Carolina's 120,000-acre Alligator River Wildlife Refuge, to protective agencies.

The results are promising. Slowly but surely, we're beginning to see a growing sense of concern about the condition of the Southeast's environment. But only with continuing efforts—and not just by a few select environmental groups and concerned citizens but by everyone—will the world awaken to the very real dangers at hand. The only question remaining is, will we be too late?

WHAT WE CAN DO

The Southeast is in trouble. Its lands are contaminated by toxic wastes. Its waters are overrun by sludge and chemicals. Its air is fouled by ozone and carcinogens. But there are things you can do to help save it. If you live in a southeastern coastal region, join a local group or national organization with a program on ocean and coastal issues. To find out more about ocean and coastal issues, consult those organizations listed on pages 54-56 in this book. Meanwhile, here are some other things for you to do.

FOR THE LAND

- Learn as much as possible about local hazardous-waste production and disposal.
- Contact your state's Public Interest Research Group for instruction booklets on how to organize a group to walk along local roadways to identify unlawful industrial dumping.
- If your community doesn't have a hazardous-waste collection program for household products, work with others to organize one.
- Ask biology, chemistry, ecology, and social studies teachers to discuss the importance of the toxic-waste issue.
- Encourage school field trips to industrial plants and hazardous-waste disposal sites.
- Contact national organizations concerned about the issue of hazardous waste and subscribe to their newsletters in order to keep up to date on recent developments and legislation.

(opposite page)
Recycling is one of the most effective ways of reducing both solid waste and environmental pollutants.

- Ask local grocery stores and supermarket chains to carry chemical-free produce.

- Dispose of hazardous chemicals and household cleaning compounds at a hazardous-waste disposal site.

- Eliminate the use of pesticides around your home.

- Contact neighborhood recycling groups, private recyclers, and national recycling organizations regarding recycling programs. If none is available, start one. For information on recycling plastics, call 1-800-542-7780 toll free.

- Organize a community pickup of recyclable materials.

- Reduce the amount of nonrecyclable materials you buy and use.

- Write your representative asking for the appointment of a full-time recycling coordinator in your state or community.

FOR THE WATER

- If you live in a coastal area, become active in local civic associations on coastal issues. Learn about current priorities, legislation, and problems pertaining to coastal issues.

- Write to the National Oceanic and Atmospheric Administration and encourage it to speed up its designation of national marine sanctuaries.

- Find out more about the U.N. Environmental Program and give it your support.

- Avoid spilling boat cleansers, paint, and anti-fouling compounds when working on the family boat.

- Write to your representative encouraging plans to set up marine reserves, places where future development is restricted or prohibited.

- Attend meetings involving such coastal issues as waste disposal in the ocean; the building of new industrial and power plants; wetlands protection; oil, gas, and mineral reserve development; and the prevention and cleanup of accidental oil spills and discharges.

- Conserve water use.

- Avoid using chemical fertilizers and weed killers.
- Dispose of boat sewage only in on-shore sanitary facilities.

IN GENERAL

- Get more information about issues related to air pollution from the Appendix in the back of this book.
- Learn more about the major sources of air pollution in your area, such as motor vehicles, power plants, industrial operations, and municipal-waste incinerators.
- Find out whether or not your state's air-quality standards meet federal regulations.
- Eat fewer animal products. They require the most energy to produce and therefore create the most air pollution.
- Save electricity by turning off unnecessary lights and appliances and turning down the air conditioner in summer.
- Volunteer for service in organizations active in preventing air pollution and in monitoring and enforcing air-quality standards.
- Join organizations promoting clean-air legislation and subscribe to their newsletters in order to keep up to date on the latest developments.
- Plant as many trees as possible around your town. They'll absorb carbon dioxide, give off oxygen, and cool buildings in summer, reducing the need for air conditioning.
- Write letters to the editors of local newspapers regarding your concern with protecting the environment.
- Find out whether your school has courses or programs relating to acid rain, smog, and wetlands protection. If not, suggest that it offer some.

The following toll-free telephone numbers provide information ranging from pesticide use to asbestos in homes; from hazardous-waste disposal to chemical-emergency preparedness.

- Asbestos Hotline (1-800-334-8571). Provides information on asbestos and asbestos abatement programs; Mon. to Fri., 8:15 a.m. to 5 p.m.

- Chemical Emergency Preparedness Program Hotline (1-800-535-0202). For information on community preparedness for chemical accidents, etc.; Mon. to Fri., 8:30 a.m. to 4:30 p.m.

- Inspector General's Whistle Blower Hotline (1-800-424-4000). For confidential reporting of EPA-related waste, fraud, abuse, or mismanagement; Mon. to Fri., 10 a.m. to 3 p.m.

- National Pesticides Telecommunications Network Hotline (1-800-858-7378). Provides information about pesticides, toxicity, management, health and environmental effects, safety practices, and cleanup and disposal; 7 days, 24 hours a day.

- National Response Center Hotline (1-800-424-8802). For reporting oil and hazardous chemical spills; 7 days, 24 hours a day.

- Superfund Hotline (1-800-424-9346). Provides Superfund information and technical assistance; Mon. to Fri., 8:30 a.m. to 4:30 p.m.

The following list includes organizations that can provide information and materials on various topics of environmental concern in the Southeast.

Acid Rain Foundation
1410 Varsity Dr.
Raleigh, NC 27606
919-828-9443

American Rivers
 Conservation Council
801 Pennsylvania Ave.
 SE
Washington, D.C. 20003
202-547-6900

American Water
 Resources Association
5410 Grosvenor Lane
Bethesda, MD 20814
301-492-8600

Center for Clean Air
 Policy
444 N. Capitol St.
Washington, D.C. 20001
202-624-7709

Center for Marine
 Conservation
1725 DeSales St. NW
Washington, D.C. 20036
202-429-5609

Citizen's Clearinghouse
 for Hazardous Wastes
P.O. Box 926
Arlington, VA 22216
703-276-7070

Citizens for Ocean Law
1601 Connecticut Ave.
 NW
Washington, D.C. 20009
202-462-3737

Coastal Management
 Division
Dept. of Natural
 Resources and
 Community
 Development
P.O. Box 27687
Raleigh, NC 27611
919-733-2293

Coastal Program
 Manager
Dept. of Environmental
 Regulation
2600 Blair Stone Rd.
Tallahassee, FL 32399
904-488-4805

Common Cause
2030 M St. NW
Washington, D.C. 20036
202-833-1200

The Conservation
 Foundation
1250 24th St. NW
Washington, D.C. 20037
202-293-4800

Council for Solid Waste
 Solutions
1275 K St. NW
Washington, D.C. 20005
202-371-5319

Council on
 Environmental Quality
722 Jackson Place NW
Washington, D.C. 20006
202-395-5750

Defenders of Wildlife
1244 19th St. NW
Washington, D.C. 20036
202-659-9510

Environmental Action
1525 New Hampshire
 Ave. NW
Washington, D.C. 20036
202-745-4870

Environmental Coalition
 for North America
1325 G St. NW
Washington, D.C. 20005
202-289-5009

Environmental Defense
 Fund
275 Park Ave. S.
New York, NY 10010
212-505-2100

Friends of the Earth
530 7th St. SE
Washington, D.C. 20003
202-543-4312

Georgia Dept. of Natural
 Resources
Floyd Towers East
205 Butler St.
Atlanta, GA 30334
404-656-3530

Greenpeace USA
1436 U St. NW
Washington, D.C. 20009
202-462-1177

Izaak Walton League
1701 N. Ft. Myer Dr.
Arlington, VA 22209
703-528-1818

Keep America Beautiful,
 Inc.
Mill River Plaza
9 W. Broad St.
Stamford, CT 06902
(Phone # unavailable)

National Association for
 Plastic Container
 Recovery
5024 Parkway Plaza
 Blvd.
Charlotte, NC 28217
704-357-3250

National Audubon
 Society
833 Third Ave.
New York, NY 10022
212-832-3200

National Clean Air
 Coalition
801 Pennsylvania Ave.
 SE
Washington, D.C. 20003
202-543-8200

National Coalition
 against the Misuse of
 Pesticides
530 7th St. SE
Washington, D.C. 20001
202-543-5450

National Coalition for
 Marine Conservation
1 Post Office Square
Boston, MA 02109
617-338-2909

National Geographic
 Society
17th and M Streets NW
Washington, D.C. 20036
202-857-7000

National Wildlife
 Federation
1412 16th St. NW
Washington, D.C. 20036
202-737-2024

The Nature Conservancy
1815 N. Lynn St.
Arlington, VA 22209
703-841-4860

North Carolina Coastal
 Federation
Route 5, Box 603
Newport, NC 28570
919-393-8185

The Oceanic Society
218 D St. SE
Washington, D.C. 20003
202-544-2600

Pamlico-Albemarle
 Study
2108 Dunhjill Dr.
Raleigh, NC 27608
919-833-4859

Pamlico-Tar River
 Foundation
P.O. Box 27687
Washington, NC 27889
919-946-7211

Sierra Club
530 Bush St.
San Francisco, CA 94108
415-981-8634

South Carolina Coastal
 Council
4280 Executive Pl. N.,
 Suite 300
Charleston, SC 29403
803-744-5830

South Carolina Wildlife
 Federation
Box 4186, Arcadian
 Plaza, Suite B-1
4949 Two Notch Rd.
Columbia, SC 29240
803-786-6419

United Nations
 Environment Program
2 U. N. Plaza
New York, NY 10022
212-963-8139

U.S. Dept. of Agriculture
Independence Ave.
 between 12th and 14th
 Streets SW
Washington, D.C. 20250
202-477-8732

U.S. Environmental
 Protection Agency
Region III (includes VA)
841 Chestnut Bldg.
Philadelphia, PA 19107
215-597-9814

U.S. Environmental
 Protection Agency
Region IV (includes FL,
 GA, NC, SC)
345 Courtland St., NE
Atlanta, GA 30365
404-874-0607

U.S. Fish and Wildlife
 Service
Dept. of the Interior
Washington, D.C. 20240
202-343-1100

U.S. Forest Service
P.O. Box 96090
Washington, D.C. 20090
202-447-3957

Wilderness Society
1400 Eye St. NW
Washington, D.C. 20005
202-842-3400

Worldwatch Institute
1776 Massachusetts Ave.
 NW
Washington, D.C. 20036
202-452-1999

World Wildlife Fund
1250 24th St. NW
Washington, D.C. 20037
202-293-4800

─── N O T E S ───

CHAPTER ONE: THE LAND WE WALK

1. David Rains Wallace, *Life in the Balance* (New York: Harcourt Brace Jovanovich, Publishers, 1987), pp. 206 - 207.
2. Ibid, p. 222.
3. Ibid, p. 49.
4. Ibid, pp. 49 - 52.
5. Jon Naar, *Design for a Livable Planet* (New York: Harper & Row, 1990), pp. 46 - 47.
6. *The Global Ecology Handbook* (Boston: Beacon Press, 1990), p. 257.
7. Naar, *Design for a Livable Planet*, p. 160.
8. Ruth Caplan, *Our Earth, Ourselves* (New York: Bantam Books, 1990), p. 214.
9. Ibid, pp. 202 - 205.
10. *The Global Ecology Handbook*, p. 270.

CHAPTER TWO: THE AIR WE BREATHE

1. Nar, *Design for a Livable Planet*, p. 78.
2. Ibid, pp. 79 - 80.
3. Caplan, *Our Earth, Ourselves*, pp. 80 - 84.
4. *The Global Ecology Handbook*, p. 226.
5. Caplan, *Our Earth, Ourselves*, p. 85.
6. Ibid, pp. 85 - 86.

CHAPTER THREE: THE WATER WE DRINK

1. David Rains Wallace, *Life in the Balance* (New York: Harcourt Brace Jovanovich, 1987), pp. 221 - 223.
2. David K. Bulloch, *The Wasted Ocean* (New York: Lyons & Burford, 1989), pp. 38 - 40.
3. Ibid, p. 53.
4. Seth H. Lubove, "Oil Drilling: It's Inevitable," *Florida Trend*, November, 1989, pp. 30 - 36.

CHAPTER FOUR: A TIME FOR ACTION

1. Naar, *Design for a Livable Planet*, p. 43.

Acid rain. Rain containing a high concentration of acids from various pollutants such as sulfur dioxide, nitrogen oxide, etc.

Air pollution. The transfer of contaminating substances into the atmosphere, usually as a result of human activities.

Algae. Primitive green plants, many of which are microscopic.

Algal bloom. A large colony of algae.

Aquatic. Of or relating to life in the water.

Atmosphere. A mass of gases surrounding the Earth.

Biological control. The use of a pest's natural predators and parasites to control its population.

Biome. A specific environment capable of supporting life.

Carcinogen. A substance known to cause cancer.

Compound. A substance with fixed composition and containing more than one element.

Drought. A prolonged period without precipitation.

Ecology. The branch of science concerned with the interrelationship of organisms and their environment.

Ecosystem. A functioning unit of the environment that includes all living organisms and physical features within a given area.

Estuary. A coastal ecosystem where fresh water and salt water meet.

Eutrophication. A natural process in which lakes gradually become too productive, often due to the introduction of growth-stimulating materials such as phosphates.

Extinction. The disappearance of an organism from Earth.

Food chain. A sequence of organisms in which each member feeds on the member below it, such as an owl, rabbit, and grass.

Fossil fuels. Various fuel materials such as coal, oil, and natural gas created from the remains of once-living organisms.

Fungus. Primitive plants such as mushrooms, blights, and rusts.

Groundwater. Water that is contained in sub-surface rock and soil formations.

Hazardous waste. The extremely dangerous by-product of civilization that, by its chemical makeup, is harmful to life.

Heavy metal. A metal such as mercury or lead that is harmful to life.

Hydrocarbon. An organic compound, such as benzene or acetylene, containing only carbon and hydrogen; often occurs in fossil fuels.

Landfill. A site for the disposal of garbage and other waste products.

Leaching. The dissolving and transporting of materials by water seeping downward through soil.

Logging. The usually commercial cutting and removal of standing timber for wood products.

Marsh. A parcel of soft, wet land.

Nuclear energy. Energy from the nucleus of an atom.

Nuclear waste. The long-lived, extremely dangerous by-product of nuclear energy or nuclear weapons production.

Ozone. A gas naturally present in the atmosphere; also, an artificially produced gas that is a major ingredient in smog.

Particulates. Extremely small bits of dust, soot, soil, etc., that may become airborne.

Pesticide. A general term for any of a large number of chemical compounds used to kill pests such as insects, weeds, fungi, bacteria, etc.

Pollution. A general term for environmental contaminants.

Recycling. The recovery and reuse of material resources.

Rock. A stonelike material usually composed of a combination of minerals.

Runoff. Water that moves across the surface of the land faster than the soil can absorb it.

Smog. A visible mixture of solid, liquid, and gaseous air pollutants that are harmful both to human beings and to the environment.

Soil. A living system of weathered rock, organic matter, air, and water in which plants grow.

Swamp. Wet, spongy land saturated with and occasionally submerged beneath water.

Toxic waste. The extremely dangerous by-product of chemical production or use.

Water pollution. The transfer of contaminating substances into water, usually as a result of human activities.

Water table. The highest level of a groundwater reservoir.

Wetlands. Land containing a high moisture content.

BIBLIOGRAPHY

"Abundance of New Life Forms Found Deep within Earth." *National Wildlife*, October/November 1988, p. 29.

As We Live and Breathe. Washington, D.C.: National Geographic Society, 1971.

Budiansky, Stephen, and Robert F. Black. "Tons and Tons of Trash and No Place To Put It." *U.S. News and World Report*, Dec. 14, 1987, pp. 58 - 62

Bulloch, David K. *The Wasted Ocean.* New York: Lyons & Burford, Publishers, 1989.

Carothers, Andre. "Living Next to the Landfill." *Greenpeace*, July/September 1987, p. 11.

Carothers, Andre. "The Death of Ellenton." *Greenpeace*, May/June 1988, p. 13.

"Drought and Wetlands Drainage Take a Heavy Toll on Many Species." *National Wildlife*, February/March 1989, p. 34.

The Earth Report. Los Angeles: Price Stern Sloan, Inc., 1988.

Grossman, Karl. *The Poison Conspiracy.* Sag Harbor, NY: The Permanent Press, 1983.

Lowrey, Leon. "Mishap & Mayhem at Bomb Plants." *Environmental Action*, November/December 1988, p. 8.

Moran, Joseph M., Michael D. Morgan, and James H. Wiersma. *An Introduction to Environmental Sciences.* Boston: Little, Brown and Company, 1973.

Peterson, Cass. "Scenic Sites under Siege." *National Wildlife*, June/July 1987, p. 44.

"Record Ozone Levels and an Acid Rain Stalemate Obscure Progress." *National Wildlife*, February/March 1989, p. 35.

Stiak, Jim. "When Toxics Reduce Recycling." *Environmental Action*, May/June 1987, p. 9.

Wagner, Richard H. *Environment and Man*. New York: W. W. Norton & Co., Inc., 1974.

Wallace, David Rains. *Life in the Balance*. New York: Harcourt Brace Jovanovich, 1987.